History in the Makin

Telling Worcester's stories tl
and zinemaking

CW01018869

An exciting year-long creative arts project encouraged worcester residents to engage with stories of their city, through a partnership between Worcestershire Archive & Archaeology Service, Worcester Cathedral's Undercroft Learning Centre, The Word Association CIC, Sugar Daddy's Café and visual artist Oliver Bliss.

Drawing from the collections in Worcestershire Archives and Worcester Cathedral's Library, facilitators Oliver Bliss, Gerard Winter-Hughes and Holly Winter-Hughes led a series of workshops using creative prompts to inspire art and discussion. These have resulted in a published anthology, joint visual arts and poetry exhibitions and a poetry map of some of Worcester's key community spaces.

This project was generously funded by Arts Council England with additional support from Worcester City Council and The Elmley Foundation.

Workshop leaders:
Creative writing and poetry, Holly Winter-Hughes, CEO of The Word Association CIC

Photography and zinemaking, Gerard Winter-Hughes, Creative Director of The Word Association CIC

Art workshops, local independent artist Oliver Bliss

We invite you to explore the inspiring creations born out of a yearlong journey into our local history and culture.

Find out how you can explore the archives and archaeology of the local area: **www.explorethepast.co.uk**

To find out more about events happening at Worcester Cathedral: **worcestercathedral.org.uk/learning/undercroft-learning-centre**

To find out more about the Worcester Cathedral Library collection: **worcestercathedrallibrary.wordpress.com**

To find out more about The Word Association's free programme of writing courses, community anthology projects and more... **www.the-word-association.com**

To find out more about Oliver's art work, upcoming events, exhibitions and workshops... **oliverbliss.blogspot.com**

Exhibition printing by **https://www.printerofdreams.com**

HISTORY IN THE MAKING

Telling Worcester's stories through
art, literature, photography and zinemaking

Produced by
The Word Association
with

BITE
POETRY
PRESS

First published in the United Kingdom in 2024.
© The Word Association 2024
Each artist has asserted their right under the Copyright,
Designs and Patents Act, 1988 to be identified as the
author of their work.

First published in the United Kingdom in 2024
by Bite Poetry Press.

www.bitepress.co.uk

ISBN 978-1-916838-72-7

First Edition

Cover art by Gerard Winter-Hughes

Design by Gerard Winter-Hughes
www.gerardhughes.co.uk

Printed and bound in the UK by Biddles, Castle House East
Winch Road, King's Lynn PE32 1SF

History in the Making

An Introduction

History is all around us and nowhere more so than in Worcestershire. But it is not always obvious how to tell that story. This project has explored how accessible the sources for local history and heritage are, primarily through investigation and exploration of archive source material. The opportunity presented by this funding has opened up archives of Worcester Cathedral, of Vesta Tilley and Laurence Housman, of local industry and migrant populations.

The innovation of local people from a range of backgrounds is evident in the artistic outcomes including drawing, poetry, creative writing and photography, showcased in an exhibition. Archives have inspired their work from their own often quite different histories and perspectives.

Our emphasis has been to encourage and inspire people to find out things for themselves, about what is around them, where they come from, who they are, and who they could be. Local archives provide a rich community resource. They can tell a story based on institutions and organisations but they also have a stories of individuals and groups of communities, just waiting to be discovered. And if these endeavours and projects inspire you to get involved, in researching amongst existing archives or adding new material, new evidence, and new histories, then the pool of resources can only grow for the benefit of the wider community in Worcestershire.

Dr Adrian Gregson

County and Diocesan Archivist
Worcestershire Archive and Archaeology Service

Breathing new life into the past through the History in the Making project

In Hilary Mantel's first Reith lecture in 2017, titled *The Day is for Living*, Mantel discusses the fallibility of memory and historical record, how two historians can draw different conclusions from the same archive, and despite there being some facts and figures, 'that offer no dispute,' there are always interpretations. Mantel says, 'As soon as we die, we enter into fiction,' and this word, fiction, indicates the work the artist or writer does to imagine, invent, and flesh out the people they discover and paint or write poetry about.

The writer or artist that uses archival material must choose what fragments of a life to expand on so they can bring that person back to life in some way. This is a dialogue between the modern day and the years sprawling backwards, a chance to view someone through a new lens, with a new voice. Each artist or writer will have a different perspective and will be fascinated by details others might overlook. The dialogue between the past and the present is deeply personal, and not only breathes life into past lives, but expresses the aims of the present-day practitioner.

History in the Making was conceived as an ambitious and inclusive project by The Word Association's Holly Winter-Hughes and Gerard Winter-Hughes, and artist Oliver Bliss, and it successfully enabled artists and writers of all abilities and confidence levels to produce excellent pieces of work. By utilising archives from within the City of Worcester's rich historical heritage, previously unheard voices were revoiced, forgotten photographs redrawn and painted into new life.

The project centred around workshops that brought people together. In those spaces everyone was able to access archival material and create in a mutually supportive and uplifting environment. During workshops run by expert art and writing facilitators, participants could learn techniques and challenge themselves into producing excellent pieces of work. During this process spontaneous conversations about the people from history that had been sourced to inspire them, would lead into discussions around marginalised voices, changing attitudes, and the reclamation of hitherto forgotten people.

The workshops felt important. There was a sense in the rooms of bringing to light people who had been preserved carefully in the archive but were currently mostly unknown and unseen. Now, the workshop participants were advocating through their art and writing to resurface these historical sleepers and let them shine out and have them sing to the public of Worcester in the 21st century.

Suddenly, an Italian prisoner of war was no longer just a detail in an archive but placed in a prominent position to allow people to really see them after all this time. A Worcester cricketer, Vanburn Holder, was transformed from a photo into a portrait, his face was carefully considered and sketched into a compelling and tender image full of emotion. This brought stories into the room around the memories of him playing, or people that knew him, and about the importance of representation for black people in sport at that time.

From archive fragments drawn from the county archives and Worcester Cathedral archives, grew art and writing that would spiral into these conversations that covered all aspects of Worcester's heritage: from working in the leather and glove industry; to preparing the Cathedral for World War II; exploring the changing spaces of the city and architectural inspiration; to notable people like Housman and Coleridge and their connection to the city. Details in images, letters, memoirs, newspapers, and more, have been brought together to inspire the workshop participants and enable these incredible conversations and discussion. So many people were brought from the archive material and brought to life in new ways. For example, Vesta Tilley's swagger and bold gender expression was expressed through art and writing that rendered her vivid for the contemporary audience and allowed new discussion about her role as a trailblazer.

The art and writing that has been produced in these sessions is incredible, but the actual time spent in workshops enabled just as valuable a commodity, namely a sense of community. This community of artists and writers are Worcestershire people and the workshops have given a new sense of identity drawn from the immense wealth of material sourced to express the history of the city and county.

Yet, it has not just been time spent peering back into the past. By holding the workshops in a mix of venues, including Worcester Cathedral Undercroft, the Hive Library, and Sugar Daddy's café, participants were reminded of past and present and future. The venues were inspiring but also working environments that could be visited again, which enables participants to return and work in those places.

This open-endedness reminds us that history is always there for us to return to, to learn from, to be inspired by, and open new dialogue and perspectives on the past. Something this project has been driven by from the start and it is a testament to facilitating workshops that bring people together to experience their city in new ways.

Ruth Stacey,
Lecturer in Creative Writing, University of Worcester
ruthstacey.com

Writing Workshops: History in the Making

In the writing workshops for The History in the Making project, we've asked ourselves... **if our city could speak, what would it say?** We've explored the history of Worcester, imagined conversation with local characters and buildings, and made space to share our own important stories.

In each of our partner venues, The Hive, The Undercroft Learning Centre at Worcester Cathedral and Sugar Daddy's Café, we've taken a moment to wonder, **what words have been held by this space?**

The Undercroft is a space to share words – once a safe space during the air raids (for sharing silence and words of comfort), and now a space for learning. The Cathedral is a place of song, prayer, silent worship, communion, community, and conversation with God. The Cathedral Library holds some remarkable texts including Sandy's Metamorphoses, and work by Samuel Pepys and Chaucer.

The Hive houses the first combined University and public library in Europe, it is also the home of a popular café, meeting rooms that hold conversations in multiple languages and song and stories from the belly of the children's library (where new words are found and treasured). The archive shows how our language has changed over the centuries, and how important it is to preserve these community stories.

We wrote pen portraits in Sugar Daddy's where people meet to plan projects, gather with friends laugh, offer support, find companionship, share words of love and community.

Next time you visit each of these venues, take a moment to think about the words that have been shared. **Which significant conversations from your own history happened in these spaces?** In each of these venues we've asked, **which of today's stories are important to preserve for future generations?**

Writing Prompts

If you'd like to write something of your own, you might like to try:

Palimpsests (inspired by the ancient texts from the Cathedral Library)

Write a three layer poem. In the first layer, write a short poem based on a space where you feel held. Write this in the centre of your page. Next add, annotation/glosses - to deepen the meaning of certain phrases or parts of your poem, and explore your personal attachment to the space. Finally, add scholia – critical/explanatory commentary – use a more distant voice, include more historic/factual information. You could use real, researched or imagined facts.

Think about your choice of language. What sort of words will you use in each section, think of each section as having different textures. Consider your use of sound, rhythm, rhyme etc.

Your Personal Museum

How can writing about objects unlock personal stories? Think of something that means something to you. It might be a pair of shoes, your first bike, an object you inherited, an unwanted gift, something you found, what you bought with your very first pay cheque... Write something that expresses the sensory detail of the object, as well as offering glimpses into the story behind it.

Writing from historic images (find an image from The Archive to inspire you)

Which image are you drawn to? What does it say about your own life? What memories come up?
Pick someone in an image. Write a list of questions you want to ask them. Imagine what their responses might be. Now ask the same questions of yourself.

Pick an image of a place. What action is about to happen? Use your imagination to bring the image to life.

Story Threads

What are the key story threads or themes in your life? (Some may be fatter than others, some may be thinner, some may have ended, some may have started later in life, some may be colourful, some worn through...)

Give each thread a question. Could this be the start of a poem?

The Character of Buildings

Write a poem about a key historic landmark in Worcester city eg The Hive / The Arches / The Old Hospital / Pitchcroft / The River / All Saints Church / The Technical College / Glovers' Needle / The Bridge / The Fountains (at The Quay) / The Porcelain Works / The Cathedral / The Elgar Statue / The Guildhall / Huntingdon Hall

You might like to start with a freewrite (quick stream of consciousness style gathering of ideas) that captures all the images/memories/feelings/thoughts/questions that come to mind when you think about your chosen landmark...

For your finished piece, you might like to consider the following...

· Does the texture of your language reflect the feeling and character of the space/structure?

· How does the work appear on the page? Will it reflect the shape of the structure or the feeling of it? (Think of line lengths and use of white space).

· Could this only be about Worcester (which words, images, details can you weave in to give a real sense of space)?

· Are you the only one who could have written this poem? (Is there much of you in there? Is it specific to your own unique experiences?)

· What metaphors can you include that capture the essence of the place, its physical characteristics and/or the feeling it gives you?

If you're interested in writing, you might like to consider attending one of our free courses, anthology projects or live events. Our courses are open to everyone, regardless of their previous writing experience. Make sure you sign up to our mailing list and explore our website to find out more: **www.the-word-association.com**

Holly Winter-Hughes
CEO and founding director, The Word Association CIC

The Word Association –
encouraging writing outside the margins

Zinemaking and Photography

What's a zine? The short answer is anything you want it to be.

Zines – abbreviated from 'Fanzine' - find their roots in the early part of the 20th Century. Science fiction fans found outlets for their own writing were limited, so they hit upon the idea of producing their own small magazines. Home made and typically with a very low print run, these early zines were distributed through fan networks via mail, or swapped at conventions.

The visual language of cut and paste and the use of copying machines – from the very early spirit copiers, through photocopying machines and into the digital/computer age – has persevered. And the low tech appeal is just as strong today. If you know how to use a Sharpie, scissors and a glue stick, you can make a zine.

The subject material of zines is as diverse as the people who make them. They can be deeply personal to mainstream – the punk scene of the late 70s took the zine to its heart, and music and musicians has always been a popular topic. If you can think of a topic or an interest, and you know where to look, you'll find a zine on the subject.

As part of History In The Making, our zine making sessions were based a selection of themes, allowing us to draw inspiration from materials in both the Worcestershire Archive & Archaeology Service and the Worcester Cathedral library. From there, participants were free to let their imaginations run wild.

Gerard Winter-Hughes
Creative director, The Word Association CIC

Granville Orange

235 Steps to Heaven
Paul Jeffery

Love is the whole fulfilling of the Law
(Desiderius Erasmus)

Inside the Cathedral both man and child seemed like tiny bubbles
floating through a stone behemoth. The girl gazed at the stained glass
windows and the laced stone and the odd ostentatious tomb with
adorable aplomb. They found at the foot of the bell tower staircase
a man collecting payment. Grandfather rummaged in his pockets
luckily finding enough to admit them to the climb up to the free air.

The spiral stone way was a delight to them both although it was steep
and winding and the child had to be helped at times. As they climbed
slowly up, the man realized that there were some people ahead and
also behind but they were all going the same way, and they were all
huffing and puffing, determined to enjoy the experience or at least
hoping for a reward for their endurance.

Several stairs up they found volunteers with two-way radios waiting
in a large anteroom. They were checking with people at the top to
ensure a smooth one-way flow. The girl child was glad of the rest as
was the man, and as they watched people descending he praised her,
for she was so small and the stairs and tower were HUGE.

As they approached the top of the tower, the man was genuinely
excited. 'We're nearly there love' he said somewhat breathlessly. 'When
we get to the top we'll see everything.'

As they stepped off the last stair and out into the late summer
sunlight, the girl child turned to him and said, 'Can we go down now
Granddad?'

Worcester Cathedral

David Steel

Shrouded by the medieval grandeur
Of the Faithful City's perpendicular temple,
The settings of ancient worship
From quire stalls of musical memory
To grave of much-derided king,
Shows themselves with growing vehemence.

From the stoic industry of the original monks
To the tribute concerts recreating the past
The place of worship reflects
The preoccupations of the age
In parallel with the standard devotion
For which the edifice was designed and
Every sabbath is constantly displayed.

The scurrying visitors from across the world,
The chattering school parties from nearer home,
Find a home for their history
In the welcoming stony walls
The seasonal finale of the Messiah
Each December eve
Unites the world of Worcester with itself.

Chloe Wilson

Held

Prisoners in 1651 in the Cathedral Church of Christ
and the Blessed Mary the Virgin
Christine Shaw

Thousands of Scotsmen and their horses
Were held prisoner – do you know what their cause is?

A handsome young lad whose name was Charles
The King of Scotland, not of England or Wales

Was fighting tooth and nail for the English crown
Trying to keep Oliver Cromwell down.

Cromwell was responsible for the death of his Dad
Charles Stuart was furious and a little bit sad.

To kill a King was beyond the pale
It is the beginning of this sorry tale

He recruited thousands of loyal clansmen
Who marched on foot: not eating often

They purloined belongings from outlying farms
Sleeping in outhouses, pigsties and barns

Charles and Oliver marched to Worcester
With all the fighting men they could muster

Charlie down the west coast, Olly down the east
As they marched on their numbers increased

Sixteen thousand men, only two thousand English
Fought on his side, Charles – about to be the extinguished

The Royalists were trapped in the city
On the 3rd of September, oh what a pity!

Outnumbered by Cromwell's thirty thousand in all
They knew that the King's men were going to fall

Crossing rivers Teme and Severn over bridges of boats
Made with pontoons which were able to float

The Battle of Worcester lasted for ten hours
Charles watched part of the action from the Cathedral Tower

In the evening he decided to run
Having fought as much as he could have done

He ran from Sudbury Gate (in the south)
Pistol in hand, heart in mouth

St Martin's Gate was in sight
He put on a spurt with all his might

A crush of beaten men slowed him down
He finally managed to get out of town

After fighting all day, always hand to hand
The Scotsmen could no longer stand

The battle lost at enormous cost
Three thousand compatriots now star-crossed

Any soldier badly wounded or dead
Thrown onto the green, this was their watershed

The stench inside the Sacred Space
Left them without pride or grace

Held as prisoners, the price for their loyalty
Sold as slaves, deported, forgotten by Royalty.

Never to see their homeland again.

WORCESTER 2024
A companion piece to Prisoners in 1651
Christine Shaw

All signs of destruction have been brushed away
The Cathedral lives on, not to fight, but to pray another day

The passage of time has cleansed signs of conflict
The Cathedral and surrounds now look perfect

King John in his tomb, died from a surfeit of lamprey
With Prince Arthur encased in his chantry

The Worcester Pilgrim lies quietly in his grave
He once shared this space with non but the brave.

The sound of horses' hooves left firmly in the past
The peace of the building can be enjoyed at last

The Ranter ranted in the camps, the full toolkit
Now the Dean preaches in peace from the pulpit.

Prayers are offered, the choir sings its sweet song
Yearning to make right so many wrongs.

Battle hymns are left on song sheets.

In the high street people hustle and bustle
There are no signs of hand-to-hand tussles.

Muskets locked away safely, swords hang on study walls
There may be some haggling at the market stalls.

Shops are clean and airy, full of merchandise
No floor coverings of hay, straw, mice (or lice)

Food is plentiful, bread white and artificial. Meat is sanitised
Tearing at meat with hands is no longer advised.

Whilst current sensibilities don't linger over 17th Century lives
Three thousand ghosts hang like smoke over those who survive.

Charles Stuart escaped through Sudbury Gate
Followed by Roundheads and words of hate

He dashed along Friar Street, New Street and more
His journey the language of beloved folk lore.

Those streets are now busy with human life
No warring struggles or examples of strife

Shops with clothes, restaurants of note
Nothing of history do they evoke

The Sudbury Gate no longer exists
The remains of one bastion still charm archaeologists

It lies underneath the Italian Boy
A hairdressers' salon – it brings women joy!

Sudbury (Sidbury) now a four-lane thoroughfare
Bears no resemblance, we cannot compare

The changes made throughout four centuries
Each a new layer of history

The gate was demolished by Victorian engineers
They caused the destruction, not Cavaliers!

They needed the space to build a canal
To make something new, so good for morale

Beyond and to the left of Sudbury Gate
There's a hill that the Royalists did create

Fort Royal the 'holy ground' of Presidents to be
Now a park with grass, plants and trees.

The venue for the annual commemorative Drumhead Service
For those men whose bones may lie just beneath the surface.

Only one thousandth of the population attend in their honour
The site of terror, pain, death and squalor.

Turn right at Sidbury towards the city of Bath
Take another right onto the river path

The confluence of the rivers Severn and Teme is reached
Here Cromwell's bridges of boats were complete

The banks are muddy from recent floods
A board tells the story, there, just where the soldiers stood.

Beyond, the battlefield, once covered in blood
Lies under silt caused by years of flood

A bridge and a bypass march over the plain
Scenes of combat never to be see again.

We owe so much to the people of that terrible time
Not only have they given us a story for me to rhyme

They lost arms, legs and many their lives
Leaving behind destitute children and distraught wives

Houses were ransacked and everything stolen (even their beds)
However most civilians were lucky to hang on to their heads.

Farmers lost their livestock and crops and died from disease
Caused by moving armies, there was much unease.

There could be so many more sad tales to tell
But a good thing came out of the battle as well.

The English Civil War enabled the first steps towards a true democracy
Now, we just have to deal with unbearable bureaucracy!

Mary Price Jenkins

Shifting History
Mary Price Jenkins

WAR – The pointless power play of the rich and privileged
We are forever in its shadow
Connected – disconnected – LOST
Jumbled thought of our own Wars – too tired to make sense of the
shadows and images of loss haunting and crowding your mind
We are exhausted now, our lives wiped out by the constant battle of
overloaded senses
This moment – NOW – alone – snatched amidst the turmoil.
Oblivious to all – the pains, memories, experiences of peers
What colour do we perceive as grief – poppies, white feathers, colours
that shout out or the darkness of colours that drag us down
Will we never learn – has history failed to shape a better future.
Will our children have to sacrifice their lives as did their forefathers
Escape across forbidden fields – Home – hand in hand we run with
our sweethearts. Transport us away, let us lie
In the arms of lovers
We long to escape – for one moment
Shed the great coat of burden
And run freely
Into the arms of lovers
Into the arms of our enemies
Armed with fear
Ammunition of our nightmares

Shattered lives, shattered minds, shattered bodies
Pieces that even an eternity will not complete
We are forever in the shadows. Death, destruction will be inevitable
We will inevitably revisit these elements of history
AGAIN, AGAIN, AGAIN
What hope – conflict is a foreign land, far from our heartland –
removed from past horrors – what awaits us
There is the fear of something WORSE
Total destruction of the human race
INEVITABLE

Mary Price Jenkins

Resilience of Worcester

DK

In the heart of England, where history's etched
A tale of resilience, a city's strength
Worcester Cathedral, standing tall and proud
Witnessed the chaos when war roared aloud

Once a sanctuary of peace and grace
It turned into a battlefield in a dangerous place
But the spirit of resilience, it did not sway
It would fight come what may

Bombs rained down, destruction in the air
But it would not despair
Its ancient walls shook, but they held their ground
A sanctuary of faith, a refuge profound

The people of Worcester, they rallied around
Protecting their cathedral, their sacred ground
They formed a human shield, united as one
Defending their history, never to be undone

In the midst of the war, destruction all around
Worcester Cathedral, a fortress, solid ground
Through the darkest of nights, it offered solace and peace
A shelter from the storm, a refuge, a release

Through the fiery inferno, it remained untouched
A beacon of hope, never to be crushed
Its ancient walls echoed with prayers of the lost
As soldiers fought bravely, no matter the cost

The stained-glass windows, shattered but not defeated
A symbol of resilience, in a world so heated
The walls may have crumbled, but the spirit remained
Worcester Cathedral, a symbol unexplained

Nowadays, the cathedral still stands tall
A testament to the strength of us all
Its beauty restored, a reminder of the past
The resilience of a city that will forever last

Covid is Lurking
Sean Brown

Each stuttering tick of old father time's pocket watch eases the
northern climes into the season of new life. Our golden luminary has
crossed the meridian and its life-giving rays have illuminated a deadly
pathogen that is rearing its head from within a virulent black cloud
that is assembling over the globe. A hidden assassin is stalking the
springtime, and it is indiscriminately stealing shadows.
But no one has told the blackthorn there is a silent killer in the
room. Its blossom quite happily carries on mingling with the green
hawthorn and decorates the burgeoning hedgerows. But you'll find
no decorative wreaths here. And no one has told the blue tit there
is a thief abroad as he labours back and forth to build his new home
between the intertwining budding branches. Mother Nature turns a
blind eye to the coming storm; she's seen it all before, she's been here
since time immemorial.

Euphoria!

Jill Gramann

It all began when I opened the letter
And immediately I felt much better,
Because what it said was – you're going to getta...
Well, I'll tell you more as this goes on.

So, I drove through the rain to this amazing place
Which used to be a theatre, but now it's a space
That's been translated at quite a pace
Into a vaccination-nation-station.

Hello, he said, my name is Ian;
Now tell me dear, how you've been feeling.
Any cough or fever, and you'll be leaving.
I'm fine, I said, and he moved me on...

Around the corner where he'd indicated
Knowing full well what was anticipated,
And really feeling, well... elated!
That today, at last, my time had come.

Hello, he said, my name is Dave;
It's only a scratch, so please be brave.
But I felt so safe in this enclave
That my sleeve rolled up and the deed was done.

The whole procedure could not have been slicker,
I floated out with my heart-shaped sticker
Knowing that thanks to Astra Zeneca
I could breathe once more, and life will go on.

57   General View of Worcester   J v

Looking at Old Glass Slides
Granville Orange

Looking at old glass slides
Of times gone by
Recorded in those bygone days
Of Worcester City
By whom, who knows?
And who knew the relevance then
(More's the pity)
Of those photographs today?
Memories to cherish,
Of places...
History in the making.
The majestic cathedral spans us all,
With centuries of congregations praying
Whilst the bells still chime
And along its banks still flows the Severn
As does time.
There we celebrate special events
With people we love
Just like you and me
Being photographed today
Yet tomorrow we will be gone,
Perhaps to heaven,
But as dead as stone
For sure long forgotten.
Yet here and now
Outside the very same cathedral,
On that riverside
Captured not on a glass slide
But on a mobile phone.

The Lost Organ

Jean Fray

An organ that is no more,
I played upon just once.
A lesson I was given,
A birthday experience.

My teacher, Adrian Lucas,
Gave the lesson just for me.
But pedals and the stops
Are still a mystery!

And at the end
He asked of me,
"Shall we play together
In perfect harmony?"

I asked to fill each corner
Of that great and ancient place.
To wake King John, long, long asleep,
With glorious sound and bass.

It was a highlight of my life
To play that instrument.
But now in choir stalls I sit,
With only pipes still present...

*(A tribute to Adrian Lucas, Organist and Director of Music,
Worcester Cathedral 1996-2011)*

Chloe Wilson

Granville Orange

Plague
Pun'kin

Growing up in a Medieval City, surrounded by buildings hundreds of years old, can make one feel simultaneously endless and insignificant.

Standing on top of Fort Royal Hill, contemplating the view, feeling like a dot in the City's history, it is natural to slip into a reverie and imagine life in 12th Century Worcester.

It is easy to feel like a Time Traveller, when faced with a Cathedral that has stood for almost 1,000 years.

When PLAGUES ravaged Europe in the 14th Century, many People turned to their Faith for comfort; some becoming fanatical, behaving irrationally and violently, using their Religious beliefs to justify their hatred and prejudices.

Some People became obsessive about their SALVATION, choosing to live modestly and piously while making large Charitable donations and Pilgrimages.

Many People turned to Hedonism, accepting their Mortality and electing to enjoy whatever time they may have on Earth in Comfort and Pleasure.

Now, looking out over this beautiful City from the perfect vantage point of Fort Royal Hill, it is easier than ever to feel like a Time Traveller; and to be certain that History repeats itself.

A Proud Standing Building

Michelle Barnes

Welcoming vibe
Approachable
Inviting inside

A warmth, security
For people in need
Protection, safety
No wanting or greed

A perfect sanctuary
A place to belong
Bringing you away from the darkness
And making you strong

A reflection of nature
You sit and breathe the cool air
A wonderful vision
You're relaxed, and without a care.

LOOK UP!

PETER MARRS

Zine by Peter Marrs

yesterday's echoes...
Zen Adeel

yesterday's echoes have reached today,

and the paint has aged

but not the words,

'i hope you have learnt your lesson'

the sour taste has sweetened,

but the words are familiar,

but now you are to teach when once you were told.

As a child of immigrants, you bear both lands...
KB

As a child of immigrants, you bear both lands,
The physical embodiment of two hands,
The infant of two strands, for to be the child of immigrants,
            your skin is stitched of two flags.

Often a physical representation of the homeland but a mental and
verbal articulation of both lands,
You are the yesterday and today in one mind,
            the tomorrow and promise of mankind.
You stand on the shoulders of elders who carry histories and victories
in skin and bone, who made home in a foreign land.

Built a colosseum of opportunity, sowed and watered community,
and because of them we stand.
My today is enabled by their work yesterday.
I carry their stories in my skin, they had no choice but to win each day
to begin and begin and begin.

Cause each day is a Monday, there is no standstill when you're trying
to build, no Friday to wait for because bills won't wait.

Because for many, this land promised work but never promised home.
Streets promised shops not illicit stop and searches.
Promised education but left out mention of intense isolation,
property vandalisation and discrimination in the classroom though.
You carry their yesterday and your today trying to navigate this space.

Because as a child of immigrants you bear both lands,
The physical embodiment of two hands,
The infant of two strands for to be the child of immigrants your skin is
stitched of two flags.

Gaynor Pritchard

Four Day Worcester Cricket
David Steel

The sonorous chiming of the bell,
The delicious variation of the pastries,
The reassuring sounds of conversation,
Even the banshee howl of the traffic,
All add up for me to an ultimate pleasure.

The furious rustling of the leaves,
The falling of the fruit,
The constant hum of discourse,
The athletic efforts of the white-clad players,
All add up for me to a constant pleasure.

The familiar pace of the day,
The rituals of the longer game,
The shouts which move the game on,
The gentle applause to instant achievement,
All add up to me as a satisfying pleasure.

The familiar anecdotes of my friend,
My corresponding reminiscences mirror
Our shared love of statistical trivia.
New additions created every day!
All add up for me to an all-consuming pleasure.

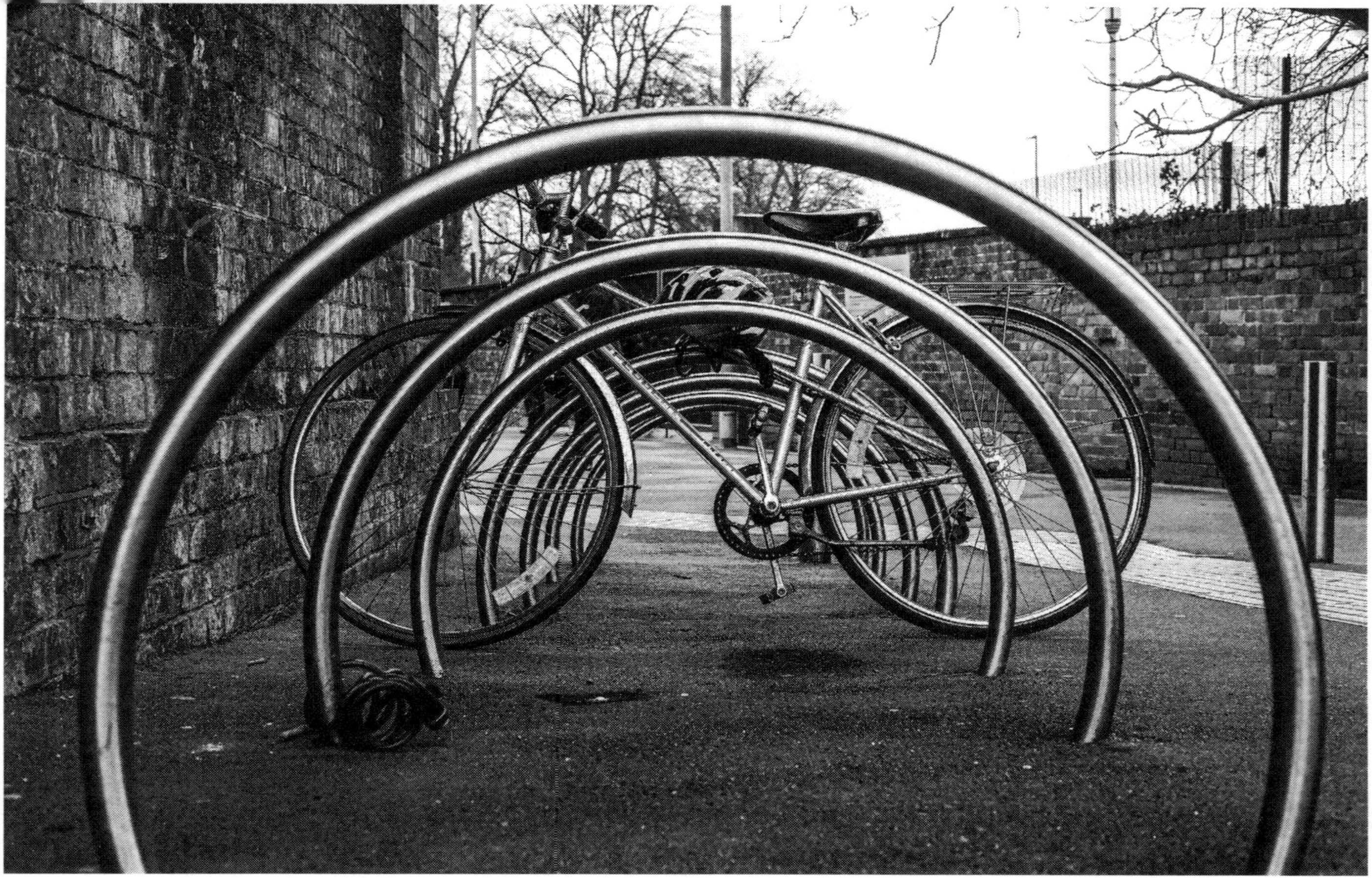

Samuel Ameyaw Yeboah

Critical Mass
Leisa

I was here just a few hours ago, full of anticipation.
How still it seems now
Before, we were all bikes and a mobility scooter,
getting ready to reclaim the streets.
Active travellers, carving out space for just one hour...
One hour of free movement, free-dom, free joy
With the crowd comes community, camaraderie, context and courage.
A critical mass with a licence to imagine a different way to be.

Rings and Needles
Leisa

Her first piercing was made here many moons ago
Just two small gold studs, shot into her ears with a gun.
It was her idea but, oh the look of shock and betrayal
she shot into my ♥
She is now adorned with rings of metal in her face
A juxtaposition, accentuating her blossoming beauty

Saving the Mother Planet
Leisa

She will rise, do what she is wont to do
For she is nature, nature is as nature does – whatcha gonna do?
And we can try to be her stewards, while we tread lightly on her skin
But, in the end, if she can do better without us, she'll remove us
By flood or famine, drought or pestilence – it was foretold.
We are raised as omnipotent
but really we are just blinded by her reflection.
If we fail, if it's already too late,
she'll survive and thrive long after we are gone.

Elgar Statue: An ode to C. Alive Roberts
Leisa

A talented writer who fell in love beneath her class with her music
class teacher
She gave up a lot and dedicated her life to nurture his difficult genius
Behind every great man...
If it wasn't for Alice...
A scholar later noted a "tincture of radicalisation" in Alice's novel,
Marchcroft Manor
I can't but help imagine that Alice would approve of this occasional
site for public protest

Dear Homeland
Eltayeb Bashar

Dear homeland,
Your children are up in arms
And I am beyond your borders,
Dear homeland,
They forced themselves upon you,
In the alleyways of your sand,
Dear homeland,
Strangers sleep in my granny's bed
And wear my uncles' clothes,
Dear homeland,
This war has made us into a nation of refugees,
Of wandering lost souls,
Taking buses to the north,
Drifting on makeshift boats,
And filling the sea with our tears,
Dear homeland,
I am beyond your borders
But you are the drum
That beats inside my shattered heart
When the night can hide my endless wailing,
Dear homeland,
I know that we will come back one day
And drink tea on your streets,
Take back our homes
And be your prodigal Children,
Don't weep homeland
You're in our hearts,
Even when you are not beneath our feet.

Homenash House
Michelle Barnes

Dear Caroline, your voice is angelic
It flows through the halls
I can hear you as I walk past each residents' door.

Hello Margaret, are you okay?
Hello John, I hope you're not in pain.
Hello Iris, I hope you're well,
Hello Ileana, so sweet... I can tell.
Hello Georgie, I hope you're fine,
Are you out with your daughter today, to dine?
Hello Al, it's nice to see you today.
Just so welcoming in every way.

Checking on them
to make sure they're fine
It might just be a job, but your voice is so kind.

I can hear your voice when I'm cleaning each frame
Making sure they're okay, not suffering with pain.
 I can see your smile, as they walk in and out
The way they adore you leaves no doubt.
 So soft and gentle, no reason to shout...

I can hear through the hallways each telephone chime
An angelic voice welcoming and kind.

BILLY
A Loving Son

No.5 Inglethorpe Square was an ordinary house in an ordinary street in Worcester. Ada Brown and her ailing husband Harry resided there with their family in their rented two up two down. Ada's loving son Billy had taken on the role of man of the house as his father's fate was already sealed from his time in the coal mines of Aberdare. His lungs were failing fast; the coal dust had taken its toll.

1914 arrived in a cloak and on the continent daggers were drawn; Europe was teetering on the brink of an abyss. Meanwhile, in the backyards of Inglethorpe Square, young Billy was wistfully reminiscing with his best pal Ernie Nokes about how their pigeons had performed the previous year and how they could make improvements to their stock for the future. How their birds were mated was to be their decision, best not to leave that to chance. Their talk turned to the rumours that there could be a war as they had seen posters, but when you're young and you're the dependable one looking after your expectant mother, sickly father and younger brother, war seems far away. Anyway, Uncle Charlie Ford had said that even if a war did start it would be all over by Christmas.

But military time ticks on at double pace and the threatened war had now become a reality. Kitchener's finger eventually finds you. Bill, older now but maybe not wiser, does not want to be left out as his peers are getting suited and booted. So, on the 9th February 1915 he proudly enlists, completes his metamorphosis and emerges as Private William John Brown 21467. He hasn't been quite truthful though as he isn't 18 yet but who will know? He bids farewell to his mother, father and sisters and then picks up his younger brother Frank and his new baby brother Benjamin and tells them, with a stern face tempered with a twinkle in his eye, to be good and he'll see them soon.

An excerpt from 'Billy - A Loving Son' zine by Sean Brown

On The Buses Together

A zine about successfully raising money without sacrificing staff, volunteers, service users, or stakeholders

'On The Buses Together' zine by John E Parman

From the Hills to the City
Nicola Longworth-Cook

*(Sometimes it's hard to leave Malvern to venture over to Worcester:
having a friendly place to go makes it worth it).*

Today the hills are broad,
Sunshine certain, blocks of solidity.
They say, "we're fine – your home is
Safe. The ones you love are
Safe. You can leave them here
In my granite arms – go."
So I swallow my hesitation, drive
Past skeleton orchards, branches bursting mistletoe
Muddied, gravid sheep grazing below.
Glimpse gap in a hedge: early Spring wheat, trembling green.
The edging of Madresfield Estate
Oak avenues leading to black and gold, closed, gates.

Through Guarlford, Callow End, the road
Dips and bends, skirts the gentle foothills,
Flattening to smooth floodplain, at Powick.
Worcester Cathedral rises sentinel,
Still distant.

Broad fields stretch, sticky with red clay.
Red as rust, red blood.
Holding dark memory scars of battle at Powick Bridge.
Where the King's men and Cromwell's
Fought and died, cousin against cousin,
Neighbours, friends, forced into opposing sides:
Nothing Civil about war.
Now circling gulls echo their cries.

Lower Wick allotments pass, packed with
Improvised sheds and bamboo canes.
New plots for the coming season.

The Town Bridge is grey with the flood-left sludge of January.
Subsiding now, the Severn still pushes past
Whole willow trees trapped broadside between stone pier and abutment.
Where the channels narrow, khaki water surges recklessly fast,

But the swans ride the flow, unconcerned.
They return to the cricket ground steps, flood wandering done
Over burst banks, paddled past Brown's –
Nearly up to the Glover's Needle this time round.

In the riverside car park
I find a silty space beneath a great viaduct arch,
Underside brickwork sooted black and streaked white with leached salts.
Empty nest holes between bricks await the house martins' return
Unafraid of heights, the aerial buddleia is budding already
Overhead the Hereford to Birmingham train's,
Shunting steel wheels rumble and screech.

I turn to walk towards town
Past concrete benches where we sat on
Hot summer days on workshop breaks, laughing, just us.
Some days the Hive is a flashy gold crown
Glinting against blue sky.
Today though she is bronze, hunkered down
Full of focus, busy study, modern industry.

Through a steel and glass mall where shiny
New shop faces appear, struggle, close the same year
Their temporary spaces soul-less, but trying so hard.
Into city pavements, paced by shoppers, or mostly
Just lookers, people momentarily disconnected,
Reflected, in Mountain Warehouse windows,
Dreaming of breaking free from their phone,
Being outdoors more.
Homeless girl in the shop doorway, ignored.

Break from the crowd into Trinity Passage,
Past retch-stinking bins
Deterring the less focussed, less determined.
To the rainbow flagged windows
Signalling safety within,
Bearded smiles and doughnuts from heaven,
Chatter and warmth and oat milk lattes,
Friends and acceptance at Sugar Daddy's.

Medhi Meirzaie

Walking Worcestershire's wonderful (waste-strewn) ways
Jill Gramann

Walking down our lane today I shed a tear;
Fast-food packaging thrown everywhere;
Nothing to be done with idiots like that, yet it's so easy!

> All you need is common sense;
> Don't sling your rubbish over the fence!
> All you need is common sense, sense; sense is all you need!

There's nothing to be chucked that can't be saved;
No reason to give Coke cans a woodland grave;
Nothing to be done with idiots like that, yet it's so easy!

> All you need is common sense;
> Fly-tipping is a statutory offence.
> All you need is common sense, sense; sense is all you need!

Without condoms (used) and countless soggy spliffs;
Our countryside would be so lovely, only if –
Something was done with idiots like that, because it's easy.

> All you need is common sense;
> Nothing to be said in self-defence!
> All you need is common sense, sense; sense is all you need!

All in a Day's Walk
Sean Brown

August is slowly but surely turning its face from summer skies, to herald the approach of autumn. The hedgerows stand in dishevelled lines, awaiting their summer coats to be pruned back. Field margins that once hosted a myriad of life are now visited only by a few fluttering cabbage whites as they search for a mate, but it's too late. Corpses of willowherb, cliff spurge and hogweed lie at the feet of bowing thistles. These once proud, upstanding sentinels bristled with barbs but are now mere skeletons of their former selves. Yet, they are determined to hold on for one last gust to take their downy seeds to a nursery bed, before Old Father Time scythes them down.

The west wind carries the bright tone of a distant church bell, ringing out God's voice as it calls the faithful. The same wind agitates the over ripe rape seeds nestling inside their pods, causing them to rattle as if to call out to the farmer to come and seal their fate. Underfoot, the remains of a clay-pipe bowl reveals itself. The recent downpours have washed away its grave coverings and exposed its resting place. It lies in a field of swaying barley, evoking memories of ancient folk who once trod these pathways. The turning earth will soon be littered with harvest detritus; stumpy corn stalks, empty seed pods and wasted ears, all awaiting the return of the gleaming plough share.

Snowdrops on Fort Royal Hill

Commanding our attention, historically, they push

Through layers of histories

Soil eroding minds, green crowns cloaked in white

Thrusting through the outer limits

Shimmering pearls of wisdom and joy

Carried forward from the depths, to onset hope

A dancing vision in frosted mists

Swarms of swaying soldiers waiting with baited breath

Catch the eye in the line of fire

Escaping the winters wrath, they stand united

Blasted by the cruel winds that sweep the hill

Defy the night, embrace the day

Welcome forth the spring

Mary Price Jenkins

A lady on a wall
Charlotte Fletcher

A lady on a wall,

Whose streaks of colours, strike us all.

Whose independent spirit is bright,

Compared to the white brick canvas, an ordinary sight,

Deprived of creativities light.

A poem to the bench
Charlotte Fletcher

You hold all our memories,
You've heard many conversations,
You've been scattered with many pastry crumbs,
Which the pigeons pick off you.
You give rest to tired feet,
Gratified to take a seat,
You're a place, where I enjoy to eat,
Watching the river.
I bet you talk to the trees, admiring the weather,
Or complaining about the rain that causes puddles,
so people don't want to be near you.
I'm sure they enjoy your company,
They'd be lost without you.
People wouldn't stop to sit and enjoy the view.

Japanese Quince In St Andrew's Garden

Christine Shaw

I am placed quietly in the corner
The gardeners do their best to keep me in order
On the crossroads twixt pedestrian crossings
I hear their conversations while they are walking
My blossom is out in full
Beautiful, even if I say so.
Day by day I continue to grow
Despite the detritus that people throw
Which gathers beneath my crown of thorns
I make the sacrifice and mourn
People who have passed me by
Not a glance do they give me, they are preoccupied

The spire above, the Glover's Needle
Just down the road from Worcester Cathedral
Was rebuilt in seventeen fifty-one
Following damage by a 'monstrous storm'
Originally built for St Andrew's church
Which was demolished according to research.
It was nicknamed to honour the population
Who made gloves and Worcester's reputation.

The tallest spire in England which is narrowly ascending
Surpasses my tiny flowers, there is no use in pretending.

Christine Shaw

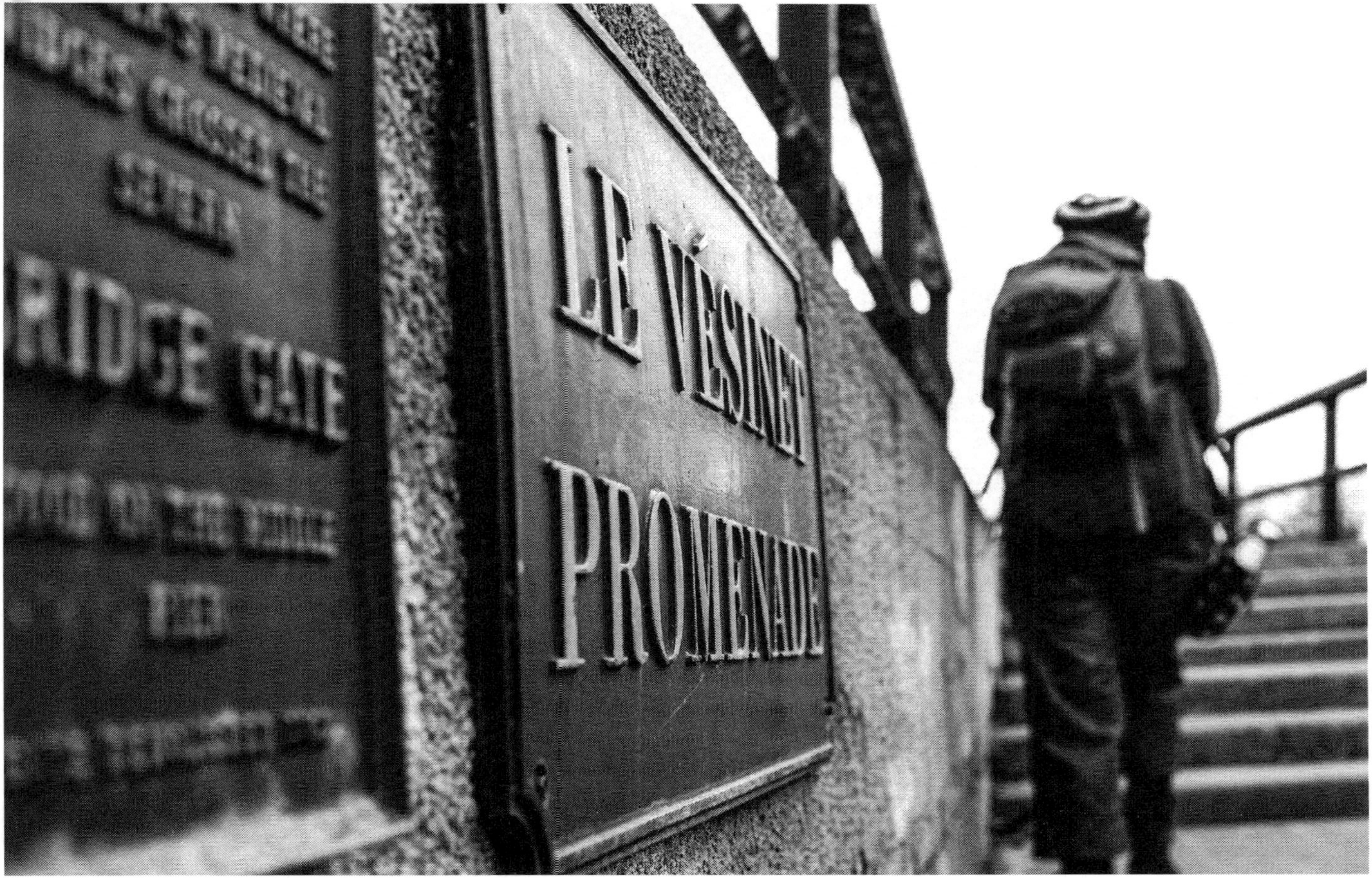

Samuel Ameyaw Yeboah

To remember is to ache, to forget is to die...
KB

To remember is to ache, to forget is to die,
And I know neither privilege

For, you have left me but never leave me
So your sight never ceases
And pain forces sight
And silence is never really silent
And you destroyed this city but I am the only witness
And the courts are vacant so there is no such thing as justice
And the hospital has emptied, darkened, there is no healing here

I'm housed on a bridge,
Where two states divide
For, you have left me but never leave me,
So,
To remember is to ache and to forget is to die,
I know neither privilege.

Solitude

Christine Shaw

The house has stopped breathing
Its lungs have been removed
Bringing to me a sense of isolation.

The stillness is unnerving, thoughts race.
I'm coping with the difference
That the loss of one person can make.

A breeze whispers through the climbing rose
It is tap, tap, tapping gently on the window and
Breaks into my reverie.

The infinity of the moment enters my chest
Making my heart somersault
With a feeling of dread.

I breathe out, muscles relaxing
Now my heart returns to its regular ticking
Like an old clock.

He is still here, but in another form
The house sighs, he is back –
I carry him with me wherever I go.

You are not a disorder, in any sense
Jo Cox

You are already your best, beautiful self. Don't believe me?

Watch your nieces and nephews and notice how they light up as their tiny fingers trace your creases and crevices, your dips and hollows. Your face is their playground. Joy is found there.

Ask your mother. Listen when she tells familiar tales of never being able to tame your wild hair. See how she laughs when she claims your hair always held promises of adventure to come.

Listen to your father proudly speak about your strong nose and follow his finger as he points out family members you share it with.

Pay attention when your friends tease you about your permanently furrowed brow. Hear the love and pride there. They understand that your trenched skin is a memorial to all you have overcome.

Ask your lover, for he will speak of your intense eyes that challenge, captivate, question, debate, light up with desire. Sense his smiling face, ready for the tickle of your striking moustache as he leans in to kiss you.

No part of you requires removal, treatment or improvement.

Your very being is a tonic, in every sense, essentially.

You are already your best, beautiful self.

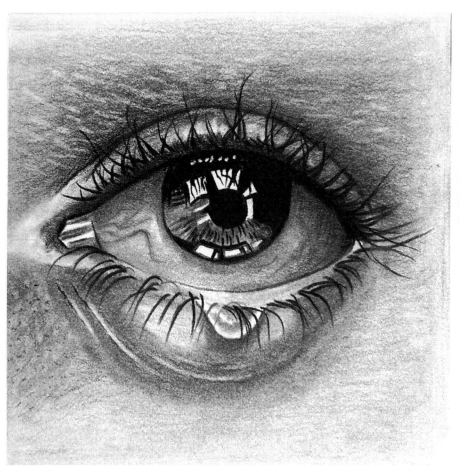

Medhi Meirzaie

Disability
Charlotte Fletcher

I feel you with everything I do
It is difficult to ignore you
And sometimes I hate you
There's a truth about you. I must speak of you,
Or I myself will be ignored, misunderstood in some way, so I speak of
you loud,
Keep away from the crowd
Of chaos and unaware existence.
You nag at me with your nagging persistence
Why through the years I've had to build up some resistance
To deal with you
Because you are true.
I am not nothing without you
But perhaps I can help others deal with it too
Be better than to sit and sulk, while those suffer more than I do.

Sugar Daddy
Leisa

Standing proud in the queer space he's created.

Strikingly beautiful and, paradoxically,

holding both strength & vulnerability in his animated hands.

My ears and my eyes are instantly engaged.

His spinning of yarns, stories interwoven with expression & energy,

Emboldened by justice and a need to build community.

Standing proud in the queer space he's created, Strikingly beautiful & Paradoxically holding both strength & vulnerability in his animated hands

My ears & my eyes are instantly engaged.

His spinning of yarns stories interwoven with expression & energy emboldened by justice and a need to build community.

TWINKLE

Leisa

King John
David Steel

That Britain's scoundrel king
Should have no place to hide
Is such a strange ironic thing.
His Worcester shrine is open wide.

Some children used to know that bad King John,
Sailed in the Wash and his bags had gone.
Young visitors who now to the library come
Will be struck by the sight of John's bony thumb.

His tomb resides in Worcester's care
And many connected things besides.
His shroud and seal recovered where
They were conserved from any decaying tides.

King John enjoys a damning reputation
From his time as Regent to his brother.
Is this legend a wronging fabrication
Owing more to the story of another?

John's movements towards a legal system
Are contrasted with his evil personal traits.
His potent issue of children, he never missed them:
While 1215 is among his famous dates.

So, Worcester's famous sleeping king
Still causes earnest debates.
Opinions vary mightily and swing
While his true legacy will be left to the fates.

Mary Price Jenkins

Personal Digest – (9 years in Worcester)
Sage White-Drake

Wondering/Wandering (2015)

The plains are bleak, the air is still.
Silent as a grave, a complete lack of will.
A spark – the sun, who knows?
Questions! Questions!

Outcast (2016)

Where did you all go?
Why did you all go?
The threat of danger, all too real
But finally, I am safe.

Repairing (2017)

The pieces stretch before me,
A jigsaw of infinite design.
Each shard looks so different,
Surely there must be a way to weave them
Into a blanket.

Community (2018)

A radiant rainbow
I'm here to support/belong
These are my tribes
I'm grateful for you all

Energy (2019)

The race is hectic
My time is filled.
I should be drained
I'm far too thrilled!

Self/Identity (2020)

A brain – a semblance of circuits
A body – seen better days, careless owner
A soul – unlabelled, unsure, emerging
A heart – broken, beating, raw...

Temporal Loss (2021)

Limbo!
Is this where I am?
Seconds, minutes, hours, days, weeks, months...
These words lose all meaning

Emergence (2022)

No more virtual disconnection
The bubbles have burst
I've missed you all
This social butterfly leaves the cocoon

Relationship (2023)

Summer. The sun shines, you shine more...
Seasonal slump, everyone becomes disconnected...
Winter permeates the heart and home
A confusing cacophony
The end? I hope not!

History
Mx. Adam Khan

History	My Personal History
From the ancient Greek verb 'to know'	Filled with adversity and marginalisation
Is why I chose to study	Is why I chose to organise
History	My Story
At university	Through my lens
Critically	Authentically
And understand	And understand
Why the world is	Why the world is
The way it is	The way it is
To learn how to make the world	To learn how to make the world
A just place	A safer space

Thursday Nachos
Jo Cox

I belong in this crowded, bustling canteen, queuing with my friends, mouth watering in anticipation of melted cheese on crispy nachos. Our Thursday tradition, necessary fuel for a long day of lectures. My eyes roam the room and I pinch myself. I'm here, I'm really doing it! The university student I never thought I could be, shoulder to shoulder with friends that I already know are for life.

I love this moment each week, a reliable reprieve in a day packed with variety; favourite lectures, favourite lecturers, and not-so favourites too. We put the world to rights, moaning about the upcoming and much dreaded presentations, comparing notes on essay progress, catching up on gossip, offering encouragement and belief to nourish each other. We soak it all in, keen to make the most of every moment, the perspective of mature students who know how quickly these years will pass.

I don't remember much about the learning, the lectures, the essays. But I can close my eyes and be transported back to that university canteen on a Thursday, can hear the chatter, the clatter, can taste those delicious, hard-worked-for nachos, can feel the joy of friendship and adventure alive in my body...

Malwina Lesniak

A Landmark in History
Mx. Adam Khan

One person's impact on the world
Means landmarks can be any form

Grandiose architecture, innovative inventions, and historical things
Are all but in the past, being bygone flings

That keepsake or trinket, holding sentimental value
A value much more than money can buy, many fold

Whether written or spoken, words telling stories
Enabling communities to reminisce their memories

That keepsake or trinket, holding sentimental value
A value much more than money can buy, many fold

Whether a practice attempt or a frustrated in contempt
Your art, in whatever form it may be, is not exempt

As your landmark in history
Is part of you for all to see

Dear Worcester

Michelle Barnes

I was born to you on that day,
Can't recall the time, but it was the 6th of May,
In the hospital where it then was stood,
I was born to you,
You were my place,
Memories of growing up,
learning to skate,
Making friends,
falling out,
But Worcester I was born to you, there's no doubt.
St Johns Worcester
My home address
Playing in the streets,
Making a den,
Riding on the milk float with Reg,
Or following the window cleaner,
Even as young as ten.
Dear Worcester,
I was born to you,
So many cherished memories I hold on too,
St Clements School when I was young,
Then Christopher Whitehead,
Which wasn't as good,
Bullied, picked on,
I'd skive if I could.
The Fox Inn Pitmaston Road,
Which was run by Auntie Lin and Uncle Ken,
Was my saviour my place to go,
Playing pool,
Singing songs,
Eating crisps and pickled eggs,
Cornish pasties were the best,
It's flats now since my Uncle died,
Nowhere to go now to flee or hide,
To feel safe when I want to be out at night,

Dear Worcester
If you only knew,
How many memories you hold on too,
The place I fell in love for the first time,
My children born,
or unfortunately people died,
You own the parks where I used to play,
When I was younger and life seemed more safe and okay,
The same parks as my children,
Now grandchildren roam,
Who now call you Worcester their home.
You've captured my tears,
You've watched me fall down,
You've watched me laugh,
You've me frown,
You've watched me do wrong,
Also do right,
You've been there day and also night,
You've held my fears and my regret,
My friendships, the people I've met.
Dear Worcester,
Part of me wants to thank you,
For the happiest memories as a child,
When both Mum and Dad were at my side,
Thankyou for the memories you hold onto,
Dear Worcester, it's all because of you.

Peter Marrs

Going, Going...

Jan Scrine

The City's historic buildings were made
Of local materials by local trades.
The Severn delivered the Cathedral's red stone
And Tudor House timbers by beast sled were drawn.
The Guildhall's red brick used the flood plains soft clays,
But the smoke from the brick kilns blighted residents' days.

Victorian transport was by canal and by rail;
Lloyds Bank's granite pillars from Aberdeen hail.
The twentieth century brought materials new –
Aluminium, chrome, plate glass – the shop windows grew
Larger and brighter to showcase new wares
To attract the visiting passers-by's stares.

There's carbon embodied in these buildings' deep core;
Demolishing, removing waste releases more.
Those concrete replacements have big carbon feet,
Gas from the limestone, manufactured with heat,
Then transported long distances, are you getting the gist?
The greenest of buildings is one that exists.

Can we refurbish, re-purpose the buildings in place?
Retaining the character of our city's face,
Cutting carbon emissions, our future to heal –
Enjoying the heritage that survives in this deal!

The Banquet
Sean Brown

As the hazy December sun lifts its head above the misty horizon a welcome shadow falls behind the gnarled apple tree and drips of melting frost fall onto the frozen ground. Blackbirds peck into the fleshy hearts of the apples that lie on the banquet table of grass beneath the wizened old tree. The weak, apologetic sun struggles to gain height as it tries to shake off the restricting shackles of ancient Newtonian theories, but can't, and is unable to reach the dizzying heights of summer and to banish Jack Frost's legacy. And then, as if by magic, more birds arrive as if summoned to the table by a cosmic pied piper. Greenfinches, blue tits and redstarts all mingle; there is no need for bent knees here proclaiming 'blackbirds matter'. From his perch, the nervously bobbing Christmas robin watches the feasting and darts off to his own reserved table where he dines alone. Then he's back... then gone again. All this banqueting will soon be over when the hazy sun is called to lower its head to rest below the western horizon... hopefully tomorrow will bring another feast.

Peter Marrs

Support Us

Thank you for your interest in this book. We hope you feel inspired, educated and curious by what you have read.

We have plans to deliver many more writing programmes and produce many more anthologies with people with mental health needs, the LGBTQ+ community and survivors of sexual abuse and domestic violence. To keep our work free for our participants and audiences, we rely on funding. If you love our work and are able to contribute a small donation, we can use it towards our next project!

Thank you so much.

https://ko-fi.com/thewordassociation

Like what you read?

Why not get involved?

We run funded writing workshops, courses and writing for wellbeing events throughout Worcestershire and beyond, and over online platforms. Feel free to email to express your interest and we'll add you to our mailing list. Alternatively, follow us on facebook and instagram: @thewordassociationcic

Part of a community group, charity or organisation who might benefit from a writing session or course? Please do get in touch and see how we can work with you. Our facilitators have experience of working with young people, vulnerable adults, at risk children, those battling addiction, offenders and survivors of sexual abuse and domestic violence.

Email info@the-word-association.com to express your interest.

www.the-word-association.com